The **Tennessee** River

by Steve Hawkes

Gareth Stevens Publishing
A WORLD ALMANAC EDUCATION GROUP COMPANY

Please visit our web site at: www.garethstevens.com
For a free color catalog describing Gareth Stevens Publishing's list of high-quality
books and multimedia programs, call 1-800-542-2595 (USA) or 1-800-387-3178
(Canada). Gareth Stevens Publishing's fax: (414) 332-3567.

Library of Congress Cataloging-in-Publication Data

Hawkes, Steve.
    The Tennessee River / by Steve Hawkes.
      p. cm. — (Rivers of North America)
    Includes bibliographical references and index.
    Contents: Calm and powerful—From source to mouth—The life of the river—
Rapids and rocks—Town and country—Places to visit—How rivers form.
    ISBN 0-8368-3763-0 (lib. bdg.)
    1. Tennessee River—Juvenile literature. [1. Tennessee River.] I. Title. II. Series.
    F217.T3H39   2003
    976.8—dc21   2003042745

This North American edition first published in 2004 by
Gareth Stevens Publishing
A World Almanac Education Group Company
330 West Olive Street, Suite 100
Milwaukee, Wisconsin 53212 USA

Original copyright © 2004 The Brown Reference Group plc. This U.S. edition copyright © 2004
by Gareth Stevens, Inc.

Author: Steve Hawkes
Editor: Tom Jackson
Consultant: Judy Wheatley Maben, Education Director, Water Education Foundation
Designer: Steve Wilson
Cartographer: Mark Walker
Picture Researcher: Clare Newman
Indexer: Kay Ollerenshaw
Managing Editor: Bridget Giles
Art Director: Dave Goodman

Gareth Stevens Editor: Betsy Rasmussen
Gareth Stevens Designer: Melissa Valuch

Picture Credits: Cover: Tennessee River seen from Lookout Mountain, Chattanooga, Tennessee. (Corbis:
David Muench)
Contents: A heron on the Tennesse River.

Key: l–left, r–right, t–top, b–bottom.
Corbis: 5b; Tony Arruza 8; Richard Cummins 29b; Jay Dickman 7; Raymond Gehman 4, 24/25, 28; Buddy
Mays 5t, 18; Joe McDonald 10, 13t; Medford Historical Society Collection 24t; David Muench 9t; Charles
E. Rotkin 23t; Tim Wright 13b; Getty Images: 15, 17r, 20; Knoxville Conservation & Visitors Bureau: 27;
National Archives: 21t; 21b NASA: 9b National Park Service: Russell Cave National Monument 14 NHPA:
Robert Erwin 11b; Peter Newark's Pictures: 16/17; PhotoDisc: Alan & Sandy Carey 12; Tennessee
Aquarium: Richard Bryant 29t; Tennessee Valley Authority: 22/23; University of North Alabama: Collier
Library Archives 19t, 19b; U.S. Army Corps of Engineers: 26; George Green 11r, 25t

Printed in the United States of America

1 2 3 4 5 6 7 8 9 07 06 05 04 03

Table of Contents

Calm and Powerful

The Tennessee River Valley was once one of the poorest regions in the United States. Today, however, the river has been transformed and produces cheap electricity for homes and businesses.

The Tennessee River forms a vital part of the thousands of miles of waterways that connect the cities of the United States. The river travels through what were once some of the poorest areas in the United States. It has played a huge part in improving the economy of towns and cities within the river's reach.

Road to Riches

More than 450 years ago, Spanish explorer Hernando de Soto led the first expedition of Europeans along the Tennessee. The river then was a sluggish stream filled with rocks and sandbanks. De Soto's men could never have imagined that the river would become a major cultural, economic, and wildlife center.

Native people used the Tennessee to travel and hunt for food, and the river was a key target for Union troops as they advanced toward the rebel heartland during the Civil

Below: *The Tennessee River flows past Chattanooga, Tennessee, one of the largest cities on the river.*

Left: *A small boat sets off across Kentucky Lake, one of the huge artificial lakes created by dams on the Tennessee River.*

The TVA has also helped increase river tourism. Leisure boating has become big business as visitors tour the river's beautiful scenery. Tourists also come to see the Tennessee River Valley's wide range of wildlife, which includes bald eagles and the world's largest community of freshwater mussels, protected by a chain of refuges. Visitors can also take in the breathtaking views of the Tennessee River Gorge and visit several historic sites.

Below: *A family dressed in rags near the Tennessee River during the Great Depression of the 1930s. A few years later, the TVA was formed to help provide jobs for the poor.*

War. In modern times, however, the river is best known as the site of one of the world's greatest irrigation and hydropower systems—the Tennessee Valley Authority (TVA).

The TVA has radically altered the shape and flow of the Tennessee River. Dams have been introduced to generate power for the region, control flooding, and allow boats to travel along the entire length of the river all year-round. The TVA produces more electricity than any other U.S. public agency. In addition, the Tennessee River powers several nuclear and fossil fuel power plants.

Tamed for Tourists

The paths of steamboats journeying the river were once blocked by a series of treacherous rapids. Thanks to the dams, the Tennessee River is now made up of wide lakes and long stretches of calm water. Commercial barges ferry products such as coal, steel, grains, and petroleum up and down the river, onto the Ohio River and beyond.

1

From Source to Mouth

Today, the Tennessee River is broad, calm, and deep. Before dams tamed it, however, the river tumbled through its mountainous surroundings over many thundering rapids.

From its headwaters in the Great Smoky Mountains, the Tennessee River cuts a great arc through four states—Tennessee, Alabama, Mississippi, and Kentucky. The river travels 886 miles (1,426 kilometers) in total, passing through several long, thin lakes created by dams.

Mountain River

The Tennessee was once home to a series of rapids, but today, it has been transformed into a calm waterway by nine dams. From its source at Knoxville, Tennessee, to its mouth near Paducah, Kentucky, where it pours into the Ohio River,

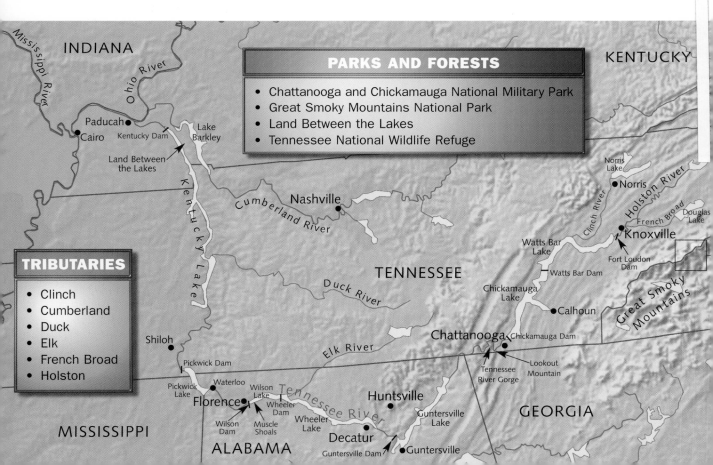

PARKS AND FORESTS

- Chattanooga and Chickamauga National Military Park
- Great Smoky Mountains National Park
- Land Between the Lakes
- Tennessee National Wildlife Refuge

TRIBUTARIES

- Clinch
- Cumberland
- Duck
- Elk
- French Broad
- Holston

INDIANA

KENTUCKY

Mississippi River

Ohio River

Paducah
Cairo
Kentucky Dam
Lake Barkley

Land Between the Lakes

Kentucky Lake

Cumberland River

Nashville

Norris Lake
Norris

Holston River

Clinch River

French Broad

Douglas Lake

Knoxville

Watts Bar Lake

Fort Loudon Dam

TENNESSEE

Duck River

Watts Bar Dam

Chickamauga Lake

Calhoun

Great Smoky Mountains

Shiloh

Chattanooga
Chickamauga Dam

Elk River

Tennessee River Gorge

Lookout Mountain

Pickwick Dam

Pickwick Lake

Waterloo
Wilson Lake

Tennessee River

Huntsville

Florence
Wilson Dam
Wheeler Dam
Muscle Shoals
Wheeler Lake

Guntersville Lake

GEORGIA

MISSISSIPPI

Decatur

Guntersville Dam
Guntersville

ALABAMA

KEY FACTS

Length:	886 miles (1,426 kilometers)
Drainage basin:	40,000 square miles (103,600 sq km)
Source:	French Broad and Holston Rivers
Mouth:	Paducah, Kentucky
Natural features:	Tennessee River Gorge, Lookout Mountain, Land Between the Lakes
Economic uses:	Hydroelectricity, irrigation, transportation, recreation
Major dams:	Chickamauga, Guntersville, Wheeler, Wilson, Pickwick, Kentucky
Major cities:	Knoxville and Chattanooga, TN; Decatur and Florence, AL; Paducah, KT

small creeks. In total, the river drains an area of more than 40,000 square miles (103,600 sq km).

After 50 miles (80 km), the river reaches Fort Loudon Dam, named for a frontier post built in 1765. This dam controls floodwater from the mountains upstream. Beyond this dam, the river meanders through more mountainous terrain, into Watts Bar Lake, and toward the Watts Bar Dam. Next, the Tennessee flows into Chickamauga Lake. This lake was created in 1940. It submerged the river port of Dallas Landing.

the Tennessee drops 513 feet (156 meters) over a staircase of locks and dams.

The Tennessee River's source, near Knoxville, is where the French Broad and Holston Rivers meet. It passes through the foothills of the Great Smoky Mountains where it is fed by many

Rapids Removed

Swinging past Harrison Bay State Park, the Tennessee reaches Chickamauga Dam.

VIRGINIA

NORTH CAROLINA

SOUTH CAROLINA

Left: *The Great Smoky Mountains of Tennessee and North Carolina are named for the mist that often hangs around their peaks.*

In 1957, this dam helped stop one of the largest floods in the river's history from covering with water the city of Chattanooga, Tennessee. Beyond Chickamauga Dam, the river flows through the spectacular scenery of the Tennessee River Gorge.

The stretch of river beyond the gorge is known as the Narrows. Before the dams tamed the river's wild waters, the Narrows were the first of three groups of perilous rapids. Teams of men would have to pull steamboats through the Narrows by rope.

Into Alabama

The Tennessee River skirts the northern border of Georgia before leaving its home state and entering Alabama. At Guntersville Lake, the river reaches the southernmost point of its great arc. From Guntersville to Florence, the Tennessee passes Wheeler and Wilson Dams, which now create a deep channel covering the once treacherous Muscle Shoals. These rocky rapids were 30 miles (48 km) long. Before the dams were built, the river at Florence was 1,500 feet (460 m) wide at times and was so shallow it was possible to cross by foot.

Downstream of Florence, the Tennessee River flows into Pickwick Lake, which is in northwestern Alabama except for a small portion in northeastern Mississippi. The lake's northern tip stretches back into Tennessee. Sevenmile Island

Right: *The Tennessee River as seen from Lookout Mountain. The states of Georgia, Tennessee, and Alabama can be seen from this high point.*

Below: *Sunset over Guntersville Lake in northern Alabama.*

in the southern part of the lake marks the lower reaches of Muscle Shoals. Pickwick Dam at the northern tip of the lake tackled the problem of Colbert Shoals, the river's final series of rapids. Before Pickwick Dam was built, the town of Waterloo, Alabama, was as far upstream as boats could travel in summer.

Lakes and Land

The Tennessee River flows roughly north for 200 miles (320 km) before reaching Kentucky Dam, the final dam on the river. Pilot Knob, the highest point in western Tennessee, is along this stretch of the river and was once a vital landmark for riverboat pilots.

Most of the river's final section is made up of the vast 184-mile- (294-km-) long Kentucky Lake—the northern point of which runs parallel with Lake Barkley on the Cumberland

Below: *A view of the mouth of the Tennessee River as seen from space.*

River. The area separating these two stretches of water is a huge protected area called Land Between the Lakes. Several rivers flow into Kentucky Lake, and a short canal joins the Tennessee and Cumberland at the northern tips of the lakes, near to the mouth of the Tennessee River. Two large towns were submerged by Kentucky Lake.

Kentucky Dam controls the flow from the Tennessee River. This in turn helps control floods on the Ohio and Mississippi Rivers. The Tennessee is nearly one-half mile (.8 km) wide when it joins the Ohio River at Owens Island near Paducah, Kentucky.

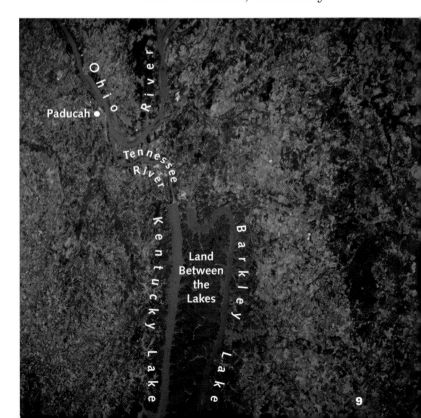

Ohio River

Paducah •

Tennessee River

Kentucky Lake

Land Between the Lakes

Barkley Lake

2 The Life of the River

Although they are artificial, the Tennessee River's lakes attract a wealth of wildlife. However, changes to the river have caused damage to some types of wildlife, such as freshwater mussels.

Despite all the changes that people have made to the Tennessee River Valley, it remains home to a great variety of wildlife. More than one hundred species of fish thrive in the Tennessee River system, while migrating birds stop off there to rest or feed.

Most of the river's course flows through Tennessee and Alabama, which have a warm and damp climate. The western part of the river is warmer and drier than the mountainous eastern zone.

The lowland areas of the river are fringed by pine and hemlock forests, while the river's mountainous forests contain azaleas, mountain laurels, and rhododendrons.

Protected Areas

Beavers, white-tailed deer, raccoons, and striped skunks live along many of the river's smaller tributaries, and venomous

Below: *A raccoon patrols through shallow water in search of food.*

copperhead snakes are also common in the region.

Three wildlife preserves beside the southern stretch of Kentucky Lake protect communities of amphibians, fish, and many land animals under the Tennessee Wildlife Nature Refuge program. Sandwiched between the Tennessee and Cumberland Rivers, the refuge, named Land Between the Lakes, provides a home for deer, birds of prey, and rodents.

National Bird

Bald eagles nest in the Land Between the Lakes. Once a year, foresters clear trees from large areas of forest in the park for the birds to nest in. Conservationists also release young eagles into the wild to help increase

Below: *A hellbender rests on the bottom of a stream. These are the largest salamanders in the Americas.*

WILDLIFE REFUGE

Each winter, more than a quarter of a million ducks and thirty thousand geese head toward a vital feeding and nesting ground beside Kentucky Lake in Tennessee. Their destination is the Tennessee National Wildlife Refuge, established in 1945. The refuge is split into three centers—Big Sandy, Duck River, and Busseltown—and consists of a range of habitats, from flooded areas (below) to thick hickory forests.

Rabbits, deer, skunks, and mink all thrive in the refuge along with the migratory birds that arrive here every year. Areas of the refuge are open daily, and half a million people visit each year to fish, hunt, or observe the wildlife.

the population of these beautiful but rare birds.

Bald eagles can also be spotted in the Cumberland Mountains around the Tennessee River Gorge, along with ospreys, another rare bird of prey. Other winged visitors to the Tennessee include great blue herons, turkey vultures, eastern bluebirds, and thousands of Canada geese. North American wood ducks are another common Tennessee River waterfowl. This brightly plumed duck roots through swampy forests and streams for insects, seeds, and snails.

River Fish

The most common fish in the river include bass, catfish, bluegills, and crappies. Crappies, known as bread-and-butter fish by fishers along the Tennessee, move from the deep lakes to shallower waters to breed.

The river's largest fish is the lake sturgeon, which is known as the king of fishes because it can weigh up to 300 pounds (136 kilograms), grows to be 8 feet (2.4 m) long, and lives for up to one hundred years. In recent years, the population of lake sturgeon has fallen. Conservationists are boosting their number by releasing many young fish raised in tanks into the river.

The mountain streams of the Tennessee Valley are also home to hellbenders—a huge type of salamander.

Below: *A bald eagle swoops over water to snatch a fish to eat. Many of these large birds live in the Tennessee River's wildlife refuges.*

Above: *A copperhead swallows a mouse. Using heat-sensitive pits on their faces, these snakes can sense prey.*

MUSSEL CONSERVATION

The Tennessee River Valley is home to a treasure trove of freshwater mussels. There are five hundred species of freshwater mussels in the world, and 130 of them live in the Tennessee River. Mussels found in the area include eelsplitters, warty-backs, and ebonyshells.

The changes to the river caused by dams and pollution from homes and farms, however, have reduced mussel populations. Divers also poach thousands of mussels, which are then sold to Japan, where their shells are used to make artificial pearls. Eleven of the Tennessee River's mussels are now thought to be extinct (gone forever) and another thirty-eight are very rare.

Conservationists (right) are working to restock protected areas of the river basin. In 1998, seven thousand adult mussels were introduced to the French Broad. With programs like this, the Tennessee River's mussels could still be saved.

3 Rapids and Rocks

The Tennessee River has seen many changes throughout history. Its Native people were forced to leave the area, and in the twentieth century, people altered the natural river completely.

The first people to live in the Tennessee River Valley are believed to have arrived at least eight thousand years ago. Excavations at Russell Cave in northern Alabama, near the Tennessee River, revealed details of the lives of people from that time.

Another ancient Native people who left their mark in the region were the Mound Builders. They settled in the lowland areas around the river's western section more than one thousand years ago.

Earthworks

Mound Builders constructed large monuments of earth as burial places and platforms to hold temples and the houses of chiefs. Thousands of mounds still stand across the United States.

Below: Native people lived in Russell Cave in northern Alabama for more than eight thousand years, leaving about 1650.

HERNANDO DE SOTO

Born to a noble family in Spain at the beginning of the sixteenth century, Hernando de Soto was raised in the Spanish colony of Panama in Central America. He went to Nicaragua on his first expedition when he was still a teenager. He also helped overthrow the Inca Empire in Peru, before the king of Spain commanded de Soto to explore North America and look for treasures. By 1540, the explorer's army had reached the Tennessee River, traveling from the present location of Chattanooga, Tennessee, to where Guntersville, Alabama, is today. He spent the winter beside Shoal Creek where Lawrenceburg, Tennessee, is today, about 40 miles (64 km) north of Florence, Alabama. The state of Tennessee has preserved de Soto's campground in Davy Crockett State Park.

Wawmanona, the largest mound on the Tennessee River, is near Florence, Alabama. This rectangular structure is as large as a football field and is more than three stories tall.

East Meets West
The mountainous areas along the eastern section of the river were occupied by several Native groups, including the Cherokee people. The Cherokee were divided into clans, including the Wolf, Deer, Bird, and Wild Potatoes clans.

The Spanish explorer Hernando de Soto paid little attention to the Native people when he entered Cherokee country in 1540. De Soto was leading the first European exploration of the Tennessee River,

Above: *Hernando de Soto rides through wetlands on his journey through what is now the southeastern United States. He died a couple of years after reaching the Tennessee River in 1540.*

traveling from where Chattanooga, Tennessee, is today to the present location of Guntersville, Alabama.

For the next two hundred years, Native settlements, for the most part, remained undisturbed in the Tennessee Valley. Life was strongly tied to the river, where Native people built most of their towns. A favorite Cherokee food was sofkee. This was made by grinding and then boiling corn. (Today, people in the region know sofkee better as grits.)

Trade Route

During the later part of the seventeenth century, the Tennessee River became a key trade route between the Mississippi River and the city of Charleston, South Carolina. Most of the early European settlers along the Tennessee came from colonies in Virginia and North Carolina. Nearly all settlements were located near the water. Conflicts between Native people and settlers occurred as the new arrivals began buying Cherokee land.

Trail of Tears

After the founding of the United States in the late eighteenth century, the Federal Government sent Indian agents to train the Cherokee to live the way Europeans did. By the nineteenth century, many Cherokees owned small farms like their non-Native neighbors, and they had established a system of government.

When gold was discovered there, many more settlers rushed to the area. In the winter of 1837, the Federal Government forced seventeen thousand Cherokee to move west to Indian Territory (now part of Oklahoma). This trek became known as the Trail of Tears, because one-third of them died along the way from cold or starvation.

Below: *A painting showing the Cherokee's Trail of Tears from Tennessee to Oklahoma.*

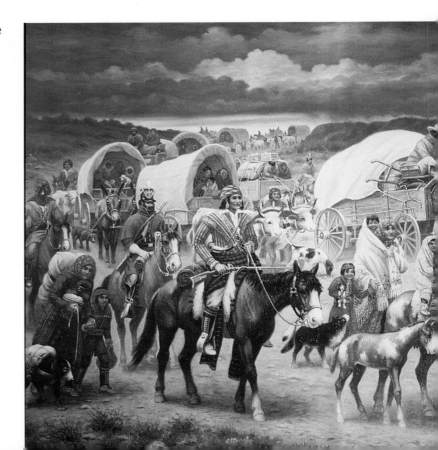

BATTLE OF CHATTANOOGA

The Civil War's Battle of Chattanooga was fought by Union and Confederate troops in the fall of 1863. Chattanooga was an important railroad center for moving troops. Union troops took the city in September 1863 after General Braxton Bragg withdrew his Confederate troops to protect positions in Georgia.

Bragg soon retook Lookout Mountain and attacked Chattanooga. During the so-called Battle Above the Clouds at the end of November, General Grant's Union troops succeeded in retaking the high points above the city, killing many Confederate soldiers. Another Union general, William Sherman, went on to use Chattanooga as a base to capture northwest Georgia, spelling the end of the rebel Confederacy.

Above: *The Battle Above the Clouds near Chattanooga, in 1863.*

Only about one thousand Cherokee managed to avoid being moved. They became known as the Eastern Band of Cherokee, and their descendants still live in the Great Smoky Mountains.

New Towns

As new settlers arrived along the river, they built many new towns. By 1791, Knoxville, Tennessee, had become the capital of the area. Paducah, at the mouth of the river in Kentucky, was named for a Native chief whose favorite camping ground was located there. Chattanooga was originally called Ross' Landing. A Native trading post for many years, it was renamed after the Cherokee had been removed from the area.

A young Italian engineer had surveyed a site at the foot of Muscle Shoals in 1818 and named it Florence, for his home city in Italy.

Tuscumbia, Alabama, across the river from Florence, was settled in 1815, and a railroad connected the town with the important port of Decatur in the 1830s. The railroad allowed steamboat cargo to bypass the river's treacherous Muscle Shoals.

River Race

By the 1820s, steamboats regularly paddled up the Tennessee River as far as Florence. The river connected with several important towns beyond, but the boats were hampered by the low water level and the rapids. In an attempt to connect with ports downstream, the government of Knoxville offered a cash prize to the first steamboat to come all the way upstream from Florence. The captain of the steamboat *Atlas* took the $680 prize in 1828. However, a new railroad became a more practical means of transportation in the 1850s, and by 1910, few steamboats were left on the river.

Civil War

Controlling the Tennessee River was a goal during the Civil War (1861–1865). Because the region did not have many roads or railroads for the forces to use, the Tennessee River provided

CHATTANOOGA CHOO CHOO

The rocks and rapids on the Tennessee River forced the people of Chattanooga to use railroads to transport their many products, such as cotton and salt. The first train arrived in the city in 1849, and the town was soon a bustling railroad center.

A small huffing and puffing wood-burning steam locomotive visited Chattanooga from Cincinnati in 1880 and was dubbed the Chattanooga Choo-Choo by a journalist. It was immortalized by the catchy song *Chattanooga Choo-Choo* played by the Glenn Miller Orchestra in 1941, which became popular during World War II (1939–1945). A replica Choo-Choo (below) is displayed in the city's Terminal Station.

Above: *A steamboat and passenger barge on the canal around Muscle Shoals near Sheffield, Alabama, in the late nineteenth century.*

Above, right: *A skiff crosses a raised section of the Muscle Shoal canal beside a railroad.*

the Union army with an invasion route into the western part of Confederate territory. Union soldiers under General Ulysses Grant drove Confederate forces out of Paducah in September 1861, and the Union army gradually began moving their gunboats upstream.

By spring the following year, Grant had reached southern Tennessee and faced the Confederate army again at Shiloh. The Battle of Shiloh was one of the biggest battles of the Civil War. General Grant was victorious, but the final number of dead on both sides reached 23,746.

Redevelopment

Once peace was achieved, the region's main problem was the obstacle formed by the Muscle Shoals. The federal government decided to build a dam there in 1916. Wilson Dam was supposed to generate electricity to produce

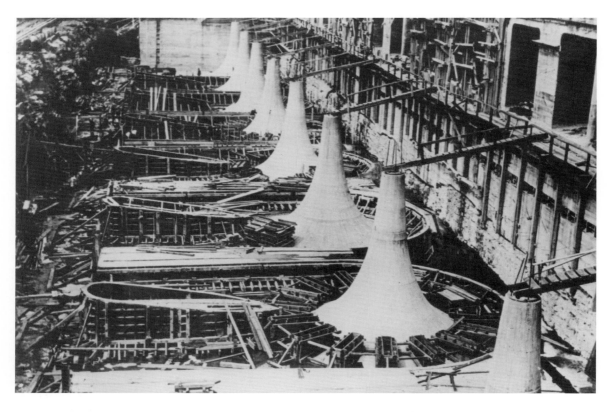

Above: *Inside Wilson Dam during its construction in the 1930s. The tall cones are turbines for making electricity.*

explosives for World War I (1914–1918), but the war ended before the facilities were completed. During the 1920s, Congress debated over what should be done with the dam. Senator George Norris of Nebraska suggested that they should build more dams to develop the Tennessee Valley.

The people of the Tennessee Valley were badly affected by the Great Depression of the 1930s. Much of the region's farmland had been eroded by too much farming, and the supply of timber was dwindling. President Franklin Roosevelt included Senator Norris's plan in his New Deal program to redevelop the country. In 1933, the Tennessee Valley Authority (TVA) was set up to improve navigation on the river, make electricity, and build flood controls.

By 1944, sixteen dams had been built across the river and its tributaries. A year later, Kentucky Dam made the river deep enough for boats to travel the length of the river all year-round. In 1949, the TVA began to build coal and steam plants to meet the growing demand for power. Work began on Land Between the Lakes in 1963 to build an outdoor recreation area.

FLOODED FARMS AND NEW TOWNS

Thousands of families across the Tennessee Valley were forced to leave their homes to make way for the reservoirs created by the TVA's dams. Many were moved to newly built towns, such as Norris in eastern Tennessee. Norris was planned to be a model community for 3,500 poor families relocated from the Clinch River Basin north of Knoxville in 1933.

The model vision mapped out for Norris never became a reality. In fact, the TVA stopped African American families from settling there. (In the South, African Americans were kept separated from whites for many years.) Many of the town's residents found work in offices in nearby Knoxville. In 1948, residents were allowed to buy their homes from the TVA.

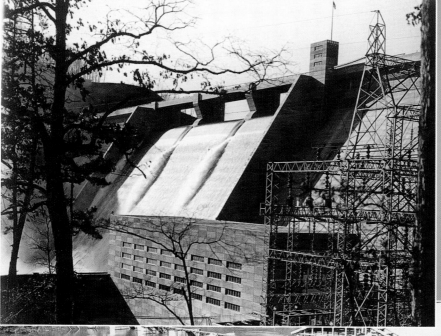

Left: *Norris Dam on the Clinch River in Tennessee, one of several dams built by the Tennessee Valley Authority.*

Below: *Workers gather before beginning construction of Norris Dam.*

4 Transforming Lives

The Tennessee River has been deepened, widened, and tamed in the last one hundred years, making it one of the most productive and useful waterways in the United States.

A view across one of the Tennessee River's many lakes, with power lines stretching across the water.

The Tennessee Valley Authority (TVA) employs thirteen thousand people who operate dams, power stations, and wildlife refuges across 80,000 square miles (207,000 sq km) in seven states. The TVA has twenty-nine hydroelectric plants. These make electricity by running river water through tunnels. Inside the tunnels, the flowing water turns fanlike turbines. The spinning motion of the turbines is used to drive electric generators. Most of these plants were built in the 1940s to power aluminum plants. Aluminum was used to make planes during World War II (1939–1945).

Only 6 percent of the TVA's electricity is produced by water-powered plants. Most is generated by coal-burning plants, which are supplied with fuel delivered by large river barges. Kingston Fossil Plant on Watts Bar Lake near Harriman, Tennessee, was the largest coal-burning power plant in the world until 1965. The rest of the power is produced at solar, wind, and natural gas plants and by three nuclear power plants, which use the heat from nuclear reactions to make electricity.

Above: *Kingston Fossil Plant on Watts Bar Lake. The plant burns coal from nearby mines and draws water from the Tennessee River.*

The Tennessee Valley Authority (TVA) was one of the most ambitious projects of President Franklin Roosevelt's New Deal. The New Deal was a huge construction program that created jobs for millions of people during the Great Depression in the 1930s.

Many Changes

The TVA's dams were built in the 1930s and 1940s, and they transformed the lives of people living in the Tennessee River Valley—at the time one of the poorest parts of the United States. Hydroelectric power plants in the dams, and, later, coal and nuclear power plants, made affordable electricity for millions of people. People began using new household appliances, such as electric ovens and refrigerators, for the first time. Just nine years after being established in 1933, the TVA was producing more electrical power than any other organization in the United States.

The TVA has changed farming techniques as well, encouraging farmers to use less chemical fertilizers and to use crops, such as alfalfa, vetch, and clover, to add nutrients to the soil. The TVA's system of dams put an end to serious flooding that often swamped towns and fields along the river. The dams also make the river deeper, and this makes it possible for barges and riverboats to travel from the source to the mouth throughout the year.

River Transport

By 1945, an open river route between the mouth and source was largely completed. The route created a thriving transport industry on the Tennessee River. Between 1933 and 1945, the amount of traffic on the Tennessee River increased times five. The river is used less for transportation today, but about thirty-four thousand barges carry more than fifty million tons of products along the river every year.

Right: *A tugboat pushes loaded barges up the Tennessee River through Kentucky.*

FIGHTIN' JOE'S LAKE

Wheeler Lake is named for General "Fightin' Joe" Wheeler (below), a former Confederate soldier and U.S. congressman who was the first to suggest using a dam to develop Muscle Shoals. The lake, between Decatur and Florence, Alabama, is created by Wheeler Dam, which, once completed in 1936, flooded 25 miles (40 km) of the shoals. The 74-mile- (118-km-) long lake is now a major tourist center, attracting about four million visitors a year who come to enjoy the scenery and wildlife.

Above: *A lock on the Tennessee River in Alabama.*

Nearly half of the cargo carried on the river is coal, which is delivered by barge to the TVA's power plants each year. Other products often shipped along the river include asphalt, grain, stone, petroleum oil, salt, and timber.

Chicken farms in North Alabama rely on the river to transport the meat they produce, and newsprint (paper used for newspapers) is shipped around the country from the Tennessee Valley. Zinc metal mined in Tennessee is shipped down the river, while steel products made in the Midwest are brought up the Tennessee River from the Ohio River.

Moving products on river barges costs less money than using trucks or trains. Many companies have moved to the Tennessee Valley in the last fifty years because of this. River barges can carry the same amount of cargo as fifteen railroad cars or sixty trucks. If the Tennessee had not been made wider and deeper by its dams, the products transported on the river would have to go by road or rail, costing more than $400 million more a year.

Barge Ports

A chain of river ports has sprung up along the river. Cargo is loaded onto and unloaded from barges at two hundred terminals. Some are owned by the TVA, while others belong to private companies. Most of the private terminals are built to handle just one kind of cargo, such as stone.

The busiest port on the Tennessee River is at Decatur, Alabama, which handles over 3.5 million

Below: *Leisure boats sail out of Guntersville Lock in Alabama.*

tons (3.2 million tonnes) of freight every year. Half of this cargo is grain, which is sent to food-processing and animal feed plants. Other major ports are located at Paducah and Calvert City in Kentucky; Florence, Muscle Shoals, and Guntersville in

Alabama; and Chattanooga and Calhoun in Tennessee.

The Tennessee River drops 513 feet (156 m) between Knoxville and Paducah, and barges must climb up and down a staircase of locks to make the journey along the river. The largest lock is at Pickwick Dam, measuring 110 feet (33.5 m) wide and 1,000 feet (304 m) long.

Fun With Boats

The number of barges on the Tennessee River has decreased since the 1950s. In place of the barges, many leisure cruisers (large, comfortable boats) now travel up and down the river. About twenty thousand leisure boats journey along the river, and this type of tourism is a growing industry in the area. In the last fifteen years, the number of marinas on the Tennessee River has doubled.

The TVA itself operates about one hundred recreation zones that have ramps for launching boats, picnic facilities, nature trails, and swimming and fishing facilities. Thousands of people work making leisure boats and providing services for the tourists, who spend more than $25 million a year to enjoy themselves on the Tennessee River.

The Sunsphere rises above the Tennessee River in Knoxville.

KNOXVILLE WORLD'S FAIR

In the summer of 1982, the people of Knoxville invited the world into their city for the World's Fair. The city hoped that the fair would encourage businesses and tourists to come to Tennessee. Twenty-two countries put on displays at the fair, which had the theme "Energy Turns the World." However, most exhibits were not about energy, but instead described the different ways of life around the world.

The fair took place at an unused rail yard, and the site was dominated by Sunsphere, a 266-foot- (81-m-) tall steel tower topped with a bronze-coated glass ball. Although several new highway and city improvements were made for the event, Knoxville's World's Fair was not a huge success, as most countries invited to put on displays decided not to come.

5 Places to Visit

The Tennessee Valley has many interesting sites. Many of the area's natural wonders have been protected from development, and several other attractions are positioned close to the river.

❶ Great Smoky Mountains National Park
A protected area of peaks in the Blue Ridge Mountains that are so named because they are usually covered by a smoky mist or haze.

❷ Dollywood, Tennessee
An entertainment park established by the country-and-western singer Dolly Parton to show off the Smoky Mountains, where she grew up.

KENTUCKY

VIRGINIA

⑩ Land Between the Lakes

Great Smoky Mountains National Park ❶

Freshwater Pearl Farm ⑨

Dollywood ❷

TENNESSEE

WEST VIRGINIA

Tennessee Aquarium

Tennessee River Gorge ⑤ ❸

SOUTH CAROLINA

④

Lookout Mountain

Wilson Dam

Space and Rocket Center

⑧

⑦

⑥ Blowing Wind Cave

GEORGIA

Tennessee River

MISSISSIPPI

ALABAMA

③ Tennessee Aquarium, Tennessee

The story of the fish, birds, and reptiles that call the Tennessee River home is told in the Tennessee Aquarium in Chattanooga. It is the largest freshwater center of this kind in the world.

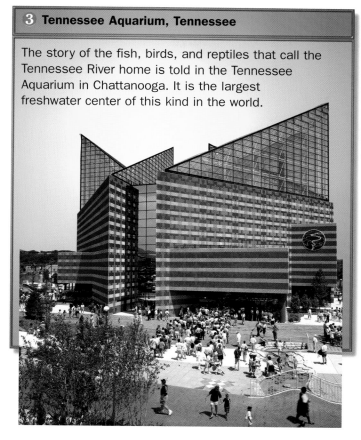

④ Lookout Mountain, Tennessee

More than 1,200 feet (366 m) above the floor of the Tennessee Valley, Lookout Mountain dominates the landscape near Chattanooga. Visitors arrive by a small funicular train to enjoy the spectacular views. Native people named the peak Chat-to-to-noog-gee, meaning "mountain rising to a point." A variation of this name was later given to the city below the mountain.

⑤ Tennessee River Gorge

This is the largest canyon on the river, cutting through the Cumberland Mountains for 26 miles (41 km). The land beside the gorge is home to more than a thousand varieties of plants, ferns, trees, grasses, and flowers.

⑥ Blowing Wind Cave, Alabama

A wildlife preserve near Guntersville Lake, close to Scottsboro, Alabama. The cave in the preserve has two entrances and is home to very rare Indiana bats.

⑦ U.S. Space & Rocket Center, Alabama

The U.S. Space and Rocket Center, in Tranquility Base, Huntsville, Alabama, (below) holds the world's greatest collection of rockets and space memorabilia anywhere. Highlights include a spacecraft simulator where visitors can try to land a lunar module on the surface of the moon.

⑧ Wilson Dam, Alabama

The first dam to be built on the Tennessee River. It was named for President Woodrow Wilson. The dam was completed in 1924 and has thirteen generators in it.

⑨ Tennessee River Freshwater Pearl Farm, Tennessee

The United States' only freshwater pearl farm. Visitors take a tour by boat to learn how the Tennessee's state gem—the freshwater pearl—is made by river mussels.

⑩ Land Between the Lakes, Tennessee and Kentucky

A 266-square-mile (688-sq-km) peninsula bordered by Lake Barkley and Kentucky Lake. The area includes a living history farm, a herd of bison, a nature center, a planetarium, and many observation areas.

How Rivers Form

Rivers have many features that are constantly changing in shape. The illustration below shows how these features are created.

Rivers flow from mountains to oceans, receiving water from rain, melting snow, and underground springs. Rivers collect their water from an area called the river basin. High mountain ridges form the divides between river basins.

Tributaries join the main river at places called confluences. Rivers flow down steep mountain slopes quickly but slow as they near the ocean and gather more water. Slow rivers have many meanders (wide turns) and often change course.

Near the mouth, levees (piles of mud) build up on the banks. The levees stop water from draining into the river, creating areas of swamp.

1 Glacier: An ice mass that melts into river water.

2 Lake: The source of many rivers; may be fed by springs or precipitation.

3 Rapids: Shallow water that flows quickly.

4 Waterfall: Formed when a river wears away softer rock, making a step in the riverbed.

5 Canyon: Formed when a river cuts a channel through rock.

6 Floodplain: A place where rivers often flood flat areas, depositing mud.

7 Oxbow lake: River bend cut off when a river changes course, leaving water behind.

8 Estuary: River mouth where river and ocean water mix together.

9 Delta: Triangular river mouth created when mud islands form, splitting the flow into several channels called distributaries.

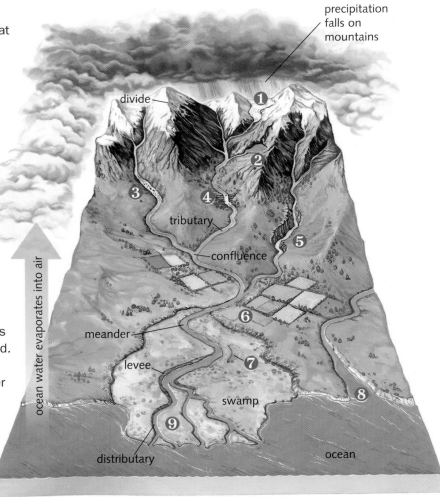

Glossary

barge A flat-bottomed boat used to transport goods and usually pulled or pushed by a tug.

basin The area drained by a river and its tributaries.

colony A group of people that settle in a new territory but remain loyal to their parent country.

confluence The place where rivers meet.

conservation Protection of natural resources and the environment.

dam A constructed barrier across a river that controls the flow of water.

freight Transported products.

freshwater Inland water that is not salty.

gorge A narrow, steep-sided valley or canyon.

hydroelectricity Electricity made by generators driven by flowing water.

industry Producing things or providing services in order to earn money.

migration A regular journey undertaken by a group of animals from one climate to another for feeding and breeding purposes.

rapids Shallow parts of a river where the water runs very fast.

reservoir An artificial lake where water is stored for later use.

shoal A shallow stretch of water, which may flow very quickly.

steel Iron metal mixed with a small amount of carbon and varying amounts of other metals to make it strong or hard-wearing.

tributary A river that flows into a larger river at a confluence.

valley A hollow channel cut by a river, usually between hills or mountains.

For Further Information

Books

Kollar, Rober and Kelly Leiter. *The Tennessee Valley: A Photographic Portrait.* University Press of Kentucky, 1998.

Parker, Steve. *Eyewitness: Pond and River.* DK Publishing, 2000.

Staub, Frank J. *America's Wetlands.* Lerner Publishing Group, 1994.

Steele, William O. *The Buffalo Knife.* Harcourt, 1990.

Web Sites

Great Smoky Mountains National Park www.nps.gov/grsm

Land Between the Lakes www.lbl.org

Tennessee River Gorge Trust www.trgt.org

Tennessee Valley Authority www.tvakids.com

Index